VEGAN COOKBOOK FOR ATHLETES

20+ Nutritious, Delicious, and Energizing Purely Vegan Recipes to Stay Healthy, Energetic, and Healthy that Both Men or Women Athletes can Easily Follow in the Vegan Cookbook for Athletes.

© **Copyright 2021 - All rights reserved.**

The content contained within this book may not be reproduced, duplicated or transmitted without direct written permission from the author or the publisher.

Under no circumstances will any blame or legal responsibility be held against the publisher, or author, for any damages, reparation, or monetary loss due to the information contained within this book. Either directly or indirectly.

Legal Notice:

This book is copyright protected. This book is only for personal use. You cannot amend, distribute, sell, use, quote or paraphrase any part, or the content within this book, without the consent of the author or publisher.

Disclaimer Notice:

Please note the information contained within this document is for educational and entertainment purposes only. All effort has been executed to present accurate, up to date, and reliable, complete information. No warranties of any kind are declared or implied. Readers acknowledge that the author is not engaging in the rendering of legal, financial, medical or professional advice. The content within this book has been derived from various sources.

Please consult a licensed professional before attempting any techniques outlined in this book. By reading this document, the reader agrees that under no circumstances is the author responsible for any losses, direct or indirect, which are incurred as a result of the use of information contained within this document, including, but not limited to, errors, omissions, or inaccuracies.

Table of Contents

Introduction -------------------------------------- 8

1. Vegetarian Cookies ---------------------------- 10
2. Kale And Grains Bowl ------------------------- 12
3. The Vegan Buddha Bowl ---------------------- 14
4. Warm And Nutty Cinnamon Quinoa ---------- 16
5. Vegetarian Protein Cookie Dough Overnight Oats -- 18
6. Chickpea Scramble ---------------------------- 20
7. High Protein Vanilla Chia Pudding ------------ 22
8. Green Protein Power Smoothie --------------- 23
9. Crazy Quick White Bean Salad --------------- 25
10. Invigorating Almond Joy Smoothie ----------- 27
11. Blueberry Muffin Quinoa Cookies ------------- 29
12. The Ultimate Vegan Protein Burrito ---------- 31
13. Quinoa Flour Tahini Brownies ----------------- 34
14. Solid Cinnamon Apple Banana Bread --------- 36
15. Vegetarian Stuffed Sweet Potatoes With Mediterranean Quinoa ---------------------------- 38
16. Spice Crusted Tofu ---------------------------- 40
17. Solid Blueberry Muffins ----------------------- 42
18. Cushy Flourless Peanut Butter Chickpea Muffins --- 44
19. Raspberry Chocolate Chip Protein Bars ------ 46
20. One Pot Vegetable Chickpea Curry ----------- 48
21. Curried Chickpea And Carrot Burgers -------- 50

22. Moroccan Chickpea Stew ---------------------- 52
23. Curry Chickpea Lettuce Wraps ---------------- 54
24. Quinoa Greek Salad With Chickpeas --------- 56
25. Simmered Vegetable Quinoa Salad ----------- 58
26. Simmered Vegetable Quinoa Salad ----------- 61
27. Tofu Roll In A Bowl ---------------------------- 63
28. Coconut Matcha Oatmeal --------------------- 65
29. No Bake High Protein Funfetti Bars ----------- 67
30. Veggie Lover Strawberry Cheese Cake ------- 69
31. Chickpea Oat Patties -------------------------- 71
32. Veggie Lover Pancakes Special -------------- 74
33. Broiled Red Pepper Pizza --------------------- 76
34. High Protein Spinach And Rice Balls ---------- 79
35. Lentil Quinoa Seed Balls ---------------------- 81
36. The Green Warrior Burger -------------------- 83
37. Messy Vegan Protein Pasta ------------------- 85
38. Tofu Scramble ------------------------------- 87
39. Sesame-Ginger Chickpea Cakes -------------- 89
40. Dalgona Whipped Matcha -------------------- 92

Conclusion --- **94**

INTRODUCTION

Athletes are in danger for coronary illness: In one examination, 44 percent of perseverance cyclists and sprinters had coronary plaques. A plant-based diet keeps athletes' hearts solid by turning around plaque, cutting down circulatory strain and cholesterol, and lessening weight.

Meat utilization and elevated cholesterol levels compound aggravation, which can bring about torment and weaken athletic execution and recuperation. Studies show that a plant-based diet may have a mitigating impact.

A plant-based diet, which is low in immersed fat and liberated from cholesterol, improves blood consistency, or thickness. That helps more oxygen arrive at the muscles, which improves athletic execution.

Plant-based diets improve blood vessel adaptability and measurement, prompting better blood stream. One investigation tracked down that even a solitary high-fat supper, including hotdog and egg McMuffins, debilitated blood vessel work for a few hours.

Contrasted and meat-eaters, individuals eating a plant-based diet get more cancer prevention agents, which help kill free revolutionaries. Free revolutionaries lead to muscle weakness, decreased athletic execution, and impeded recuperation.

Plant-based diets, which are ordinarily low in fat and high in fiber, can decrease muscle versus fat. Diminished muscle versus fat is related with expanded vigorous limit—or the capacity to utilize oxygen to fuel work out. Studies show that athletes on a plant-based diet increment their VO2 max—the most extreme measure of oxygen they can use during serious exercise—prompting better perseverance.

1. Vegetarian Cookies

Makes: 12 monster treats (or 24 customary treats) | Time: 15 minutes to prepare, | 30 minutes to heat

Fixings
- 4 cups (385 g) older style moved oats
- 1½ cups (225 g) entire wheat flour
- 1 teaspoon heating powder
- ½ teaspoon salt
- 3 ready bananas
- 1 cup (200 g) crude sugar or coconut sugar
- 1/3 cup (80 ml) coconut oil (OF: coconut margarine)
- ¼ cup in addition to 2 tablespoons (90 ml) water
- 2 tablespoons chia seeds or ground flaxseeds
- 2 teaspoons vanilla concentrate
- 1 cup (225 g) dull chocolate chips
- 1 cup (120 g) crude pecan pieces
- ½ cup (75 g) crude sunflower seeds

- ½ cup (40 g) unsweetened destroyed coconut, discretionary

Guidance

1. Preheat the stove to 350°F (180°C). Line two preparing sheets with material paper.
2. Place 2 cups (195 g) of the oats in a food processor or blender and heartbeat until they are finely ground. Move to a huge bowl and add the flour, preparing powder, salt, and remaining oats.
3. Combine the bananas, sugar, oil, water, chia seeds, and vanilla in the blender or food processor. Add to the oat combination and mix with a durable wooden spoon until consolidated. Add the chocolate chips, pecans, sunflower seeds, and coconut.
4. With wet hands, structure about ½ cup (60 g) mixture into balls for monster treats, about ¼ cup (30 g) batter for ordinary treats. (There ought to be 6 balls on each preparing sheet if making goliath treats.) Flatten them to ¾ to 1 inch (2 to 2.5 cm) thick.
5. Bake for 30 minutes, or until brilliant earthy colored. Permit to cool totally prior to eliminating from the heating sheets. Store in a hermetically sealed compartment for as long as multi week or freeze for as long as 3 months. Enclose by material paper for in a hurry eating.

2. Kale and Grains Bowl

Planning Time 10 minutes | Cook Time 25 minutes | Complete Time 35 minutes | 3 servings

FIXINGS
- cooked quinoa or earthy colored rice, cold or warm, as wanted (2 cups)
- chopped kale leaves, crude or steamed, or child spinach leaves (3 cups)
- cubed and cooked yam (2 cups)
- black beans, washed and depleted (1 15-ounce can)
- chopped chime pepper (1 cup)
- mango lumps, new or frozen (3/4 cup)
- Hemp seeds (2 tbsp.)
- Freshly crushed lime juice or red wine vinegar (2 tbsp.)
- Chopped shallots or 1 tbsp. of the white bit of a green onion (1/2 tbsp.)
- Dijon mustard (1/2 tsp.)
- Sea salt (1/2 tsp.)

- freshly ground dark pepper (to taste)
- Water, discretionary (1/4 cup + 2-3 tsp.)
- Coconut nectar or unadulterated maple syrup (1-2 tbsp.)

Bearings

1. In three dishes, orchestrate around equivalent measures of the quinoa or rice, kale or spinach, yam, dark beans, and ringer pepper.
2. Drizzle on your preferred dressing. Note: If utilizing crude kale, it's helpful to separate it by rubbing it. Subsequent to tearing the leaves from the tail, sprinkle them with salt and utilize your hands to rub and "back rub" them briefly. On the other hand, you can steam the leaves for one moment to mellow.
3. In a blender, consolidate the mango, hemp, lime juice or vinegar, shallots or green onion, mustard, salt, pepper, 1/4 cup of the water, and 1 tablespoon of the nectar or syrup. Puree until exceptionally smooth.
4. Taste, and add the leftover 2 to 3 tablespoons water to thin (whenever wanted) and the excess 1 tablespoon nectar or syrup, to taste. In the event that you'd prefer to combine this dressing for certain fiery food varieties or add an additional punch of flavor, have a go at adding 1 to 2 tablespoons of cleaved cilantro or basil while pureeing.

3. The Vegan Buddha Bowl

Planning Time 15 minutes | Cook Time 25 minutes | Absolute Time 40 minutes | Servings 2

Fixings
- Quinoa
- 1 Cup Quinoa washed
- 2 Cups Water
- Chickpeas
- 1 1/2 Cups Cooked Chickpeas
- Drizzle Olive Oil or other nonpartisan oil
- 1/2 Tsp. Salt
- 1/2 Tsp. Smoked Paprika
- 1 Tsp. Chili Powder
- 1/8 Tsp. Turmeric
- 1/2 Tsp. Oregano
- Red Pepper Sauce
- 1 Red Bell Pepper ribs and seeds eliminated
- 2 Tabs Olive Oil or other unbiased oil
- Juice from 1/2 Lemon or more to taste

- 1/2 Tsp. Pepper
- 1/2 Tsp. Salt
- 1/2 Tsp. Paprika
- 1/4 Cup Fresh Cilantro
- All the other things
- Mixed Greens
- An Avocado
- Sesame Seeds for Garnish

Guidelines
1. Start by cooking the quinoa. Heat 2 cups water to the point of boiling, at that point add quinoa. Stew for around 15 minutes until all water is ingested. At the point when done, eliminate from warmth and save covered for around 10 minutes so quinoa can ingest any abundance water.
2. Preheat broiler to 425. In a bowl, throw chickpeas, oil, and flavors until chickpeas are uniformly covered. On a preparing sheet fixed with material paper, heat chickpeas for 15-20 minutes or until wanted doneness is reached. At the point when done, eliminate from stove and let cool.
3. To make red pepper dressing, add all dressing fixings to a blender (not a food processor) and mix on high until smooth. Taste, and change flavors to your inclination.
4. Finally, amass the Buddha bowls. In two dishes, add quinoa, blended greens, avocado, and chickpeas. Shower everything with red pepper sauce, and sprinkle with sesame seeds. Enjoy!

4. Warm and Nutty Cinnamon Quinoa

Planning Time 10 minutes | Cook Time 25 minutes | Complete Time 35 minutes | Servings 2

Fixings
- 1 cup natural 1% low fat milk
- 1 cup water
- 1 cup natural quinoa, (hs note: wash quinoa)
- 2 cups new blackberries, natural liked
- 1/2 teaspoon ground cinnamon
- 1/3 cup hacked walnuts, toasted
- 4 teaspoons natural agave nectar, for example, Madhava brand

Guidance
1. Combine milk, water and quinoa in a medium pot.
2. Bring to a bubble over high warmth. Decrease warmth to medium-low; cover and stew 15 minutes or until the majority of the fluid is ingested.
3. Turn off heat; let stand covered 5 minutes.
4. Stir in blackberries and cinnamon; move to four dishes and top with walnuts.
5. Drizzle 1 teaspoon agave nectar over each serving.

5. Vegetarian Protein Cookie Dough Overnight Oats

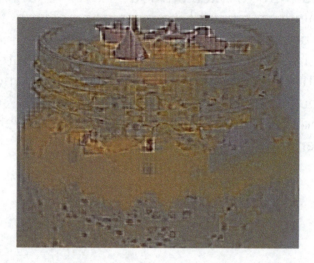

Planning Time: 5 minutes | Drench Time: 5 hours | Absolute Time: 5 hours 5 minutes

Fixings
- 1/2 cup gluten free moved oats
- 1 tablespoon chia seeds
- 2 tablespoons vegetarian/plant-based vanilla protein powder
- 1 tablespoon unadulterated maple syrup
- 3/4 cup unsweetened vanilla almond milk
- 1 tablespoon normal cashew margarine
- 1-2 tablespoons small scale dim chocolate chips (non-dairy)

Guidelines
1. In a bowl or container add the oats, chia seeds, protein powder, maple syrup, and almond milk.

2. Mix well to join.
3. Place the container in the cooler and leave for the time being or 5 hours at the very least.
4. In the morning, prior to eating, mix in the cashew margarine and the dim chocolate chips.
5. Drizzle with a little unadulterated maple syrup.
6. Dig in!

6. Chickpea Scramble

Prep Time: 5 minutes | Cook Time: 10 minutes | Total Time: 15 minutes | Yield: 3 servings

Fixings
- 1 tablespoon olive oil
- 1/4 cup diced onion
- 1/4 cup diced ringer pepper
- 1 tablespoon nourishing yeast
- 1/2 teaspoon gentle bean stew powder
- 1/4 teaspoon turmeric
- 1/eighth teaspoon smoked paprika
- 1/4 teaspoon salt
- 1 1/2 cup chickpeas, crushed softly until about portion of the chickpeas are separated and the other half are entirety
- 1 tomato, hacked
- 1/3 cup vegetable stock

Directions
1. Heat the oil in a skillet over medium warmth. Include the onion and ringer pepper. Sauté until delicate, around 3-5 minutes.
2. Add in the healthful yeast, stew powder, turmeric, paprika, and salt. Sauté for one more moment until the flavors are fragrant.
3. Add the chickpeas, tomato and stock into the skillet. Bring the blend up to a stew and cook, until the chickpeas are velvety, around 3-5 minutes. Appreciate!

7. High Protein Vanilla Chia Pudding

Planning Time 5 minutes | All out Time 2 hours 5 minutes | Servings 1

Fixings
- 1/4 cup cooked quinoa
- 2 tablespoons chia seeds
- 2 tablespoons hemp hearts
- 1/4 teaspoon vanilla powder
- Dash of stevia or utilize 2 tablespoons maple syrup
- Pinch of cinnamon
- 3/4 cup cashew milk or milk of decision

Guidelines
1. Add all fixings to a container and mix together.
2. Tighten top and spot chia pudding in the ice chest to set, around 2 hours (or more).
3. Remove and top with wanted garnishes. Appreciate!

8. Green Protein Power Smoothie

Planning Time 10 minutes | Blending Time 10 minutes | Absolute Time 20 minutes | Servings 2

Fixings:
- 2 cup (250 ml) unsweetened almond milk
- 2 ready banana, frozen
- ½ cup (125 ml) cleaved mango, frozen
- 1-2 enormous modest bunches of infant spinach
- ¼ cup (60 ml) pumpkin seeds (Pepita seeds)
- 2 tbsp. (30 ml) hemp hearts (hulled hemp seeds)
- optional: ½ scoop (approx. 30ml) vanilla protein powder + ¼ cup (60ml) water

Headings:
1. In a blender (or enormous tumbler in case you're utilizing a submersion blender) layer the spinach, banana, mango, pumpkin seeds, and hemp hearts.
2. Add the almond milk and mix until smooth.
3. I utilize a modest 15$ submersion blender and I mix this smoothie for around 2 minutes (in length enough to mix the pumpkin seeds incredibly smooth.)

9. Crazy Quick White Bean Salad

Time 10 minutes | Planning Time 10 minutes | Complete Time 10 minutes | Serving's 2

Fixings
- 1 can white beans (1 can = 15.5 oz./435 g)
- 1 red onion
- 4 sun-dried tomatoes in oil
- 1 ringer pepper, red
- 2 tbsp. olive oil
- 1 tbsp. lemon juice
- 1 little modest bunch parsley, new
- 1 little small bunch cilantro/coriander, new
- salt
- pepper
- Optional:
- 2 cuts wholemeal bread

Guidelines
1. Wash the beans and let water channel.
2. Dice onion into little pieces.
3. Wash ringer pepper, cut into little pieces also.
4. Add parsley and cilantro.
5. Cut the dried tomatoes in little strips.
6. Throw everything into a major bowl, add the olive oil, lemon squeeze and polish it off with some salt and pepper.
7. Optional:
8. Add some toasted whole meal bread.

10. Invigorating Almond Joy Smoothie

Prep Time 10 minutes | Complete Time 10 minutes | Servings 1

Fixings
- 1/2 cup coconut milk
- 1/2 cup coconut water
- 1 cup spinach
- 1 tablespoon almond spread
- 2 tablespoons crude cacao
- 1 teaspoon maca powder
- 1 teaspoon ground cinnamon
- 1 frozen banana
- 1/4 cup cooked quinoa (or 1 scoop protein powder)
- Coconut chips cacao nibs + shaved chocolate to decorate

Directions
1. Add all fixings in the request recorded (less garnishes) to a blender. Mix on high until smooth and velvety.
2. Pour into glasses, embellish with coconut chips and cacao nibs whenever wanted. Appreciate!

11. Blueberry Muffin Quinoa Cookies

Planning Time 10 minutes | Cook Time 18 minutes | All out Time 28 minutes | Servings 16

Fixings
- 1 flax egg 1 tablespoon flaxseed feast + 3 tablespoons water
- ½ cup cashew margarine or nut/seed spread of decision
- ¼ cup unadulterated maple syrup
- 1 medium banana pounded
- 1 teaspoon vanilla concentrate
- ½ cup moved oats
- ½ cup quinoa drops
- 1 teaspoon heating powder
- 1 teaspoon cinnamon
- ½ teaspoon nutmeg
- ¼ teaspoon salt
- ½ cup new or frozen blueberries

Guidelines

1. Preheat broiler to 350 degrees F. Line a preparing sheet with material paper and put away.
2. Whisk together the flaxseed feast and water, and put away.
3. Beat together cashew margarine, syrup, banana and vanilla in a huge bowl. Add flax egg and blend to consolidate.
4. Pour in oats, quinoa drops, preparing powder, flavors and salt to the bowl and mix together. Crease in the blueberries.
5. Drop 2 tablespoons of mixture onto the preparing sheet and rehash until no batter remains.
6. Bake treats on focus rack for 15 - 18 minutes until edges are brilliant earthy colored. Eliminate and let cool on the search for gold minutes at that point move to a wire rack and cool totally.
7. Enjoy at room temp or somewhat warmed in a microwave.

12. The Ultimate Vegan Protein Burrito

Planning Time 20 minutes | Cook Time 20 minutes | All out Time 40 minutes | Servings 4

Fixings
- For the Quinoa
- ¾ cup white quinoa, completely flushed
- 1 ½ cups water
- ¼ teaspoon ocean salt
- 1 can dark beans, depleted and flushed
- ¼ cup slashed new cilantro
- 3 tablespoons lime juice
- 3 tablespoons hemp seeds
- ¼-1/2 teaspoon ocean salt, to taste
- Freshly ground dark pepper, to taste
- For Kale
- 3 cups destemmed and slashed kale
- 1 tablespoon lime juice
- ½ tablespoon olive oil
- Sea salt, to taste

- Freshly ground dark pepper, to taste
- For the Pico de Gallo
- 1 cup quartered cherry tomatoes
- ¼ cup finely diced red onion
- 2 tablespoons cleaved cilantro
- Sea salt, to taste
- For the Guacamole
- 1 ready avocado, split, pitted, and stripped
- 1 lime, squeezed
- Sea salt, to taste
- Extra Ingredients
- 4 huge grew grain or without gluten tortillas

Directions
1. **For the Quinoa**
2. Add the quinoa and water to a little pot with ¼ teaspoon ocean salt. Warmth over medium-high warmth until bubbling. Decrease warmth, cover, and stew for 10-14 minutes or until quinoa is delicate and clear. Cushion with a fork and move to an enormous bowl.
3. Add the dark beans, hacked cilantro, lime juice, hemp seeds, ocean salt, and dark pepper to the quinoa and mix. Put away.
4. **For the Kale**
5. Add the cleaved kale, lime juice, olive oil, and ocean salt to a bowl and back rub the kale for 2-3 minutes or until delicate. Put away.
6. **For the Pico de Gallo**
7. Add the cherry tomatoes, red onion, cilantro, and ocean salt to a bowl and mix to join. Put away.
8. **For the Guacamole**

9. Scoop the substance of the avocado into a little bowl alongside the juice of one lime and ocean salt, to taste. Utilize the rear of a fork to crush the avocado to wanted consistency. Put away.
10. To Assemble the Burritos
11. Lay one tortilla level on a spotless work surface. Fill the tortilla with the quinoa blend, Pico de Gallo, guacamole, and kale. Start rolling the burrito away from you, being certain to wrap the sides up as you go. Cut down the middle and serve right away. Rehash.
12. Refrigerate extras in discrete sealed shut holders.

13. Quinoa Flour Tahini Brownies

Planning Time 5 minutes | Cook Time 23 minutes | All out Time 27 minutes | Servings 16

Fixings
- 1/4 cup pounded banana (around 1 little or natural product puree of decision)
- 1/4 cup pounded avocado (or more banana)
- 1/2 cup tahini (ideally simmered)
- 1/2 cup coconut sugar
- 2 flax eggs 2 tbsp. flaxseed feast + 5 tbsp. water
- 1 teaspoon vanilla concentrate discretionary
- 2/3 cups toasted quinoa flour
- 1/4 cup crude cacao
- 1/2 teaspoon heating pop
- Pinch of ocean salt
- 1/3 cup dim chocolate chips
- Maldon ocean salt and crude cacao to decorate

Directions
1. Preheat stove to 350 degrees F. Line a 8 x 8 heating dish with material and put away.
2. Beat together banana, avocado, tahini, sugar, eggs and vanilla until smooth and rich.
3. Add to quinoa flour, crude cacao, preparing pop and salt, blending until consolidated. Overlay in chocolate chips.
4. Transfer player to the readied heating skillet. Press it into the edges of the dish utilizing wet hands or a baked good roller. Heat on the middle rack for 20 – 24 minutes.
5. Remove from the broiler and let the brownies cool in skillet totally prior to cutting into squares. (*very significant or they'll be crumbly!!*)
6. Store in a fixed, water/air proof holder for ideal fudginess.

14. Solid Cinnamon Apple Banana Bread

Planning Time 10 minutes | Cook Time 45 minutes | All out Time 55 minutes | Servings 16

Fixings
- 1 1/2 cups whitened almond flour
- 1/2 cup quinoa flour
- 1/4 cup flaxseed feast
- 2 tablespoons coconut sugar
- 2 tablespoon coconut flour
- 2 teaspoons cinnamon
- 1/2 teaspoon heating pop
- 1/4 teaspoon salt
- 3 enormous eggs
- 1/2 cup pounded banana around 1 medium
- 1 tablespoon olive oil or oil of decision
- 3 tablespoons maple syrup or fluid sugar of decision
- 1 tablespoon apple juice vinegar

- 1 teaspoon vanilla concentrate
- 1 cup destroyed apple
- 1/2 cup hacked walnuts
- 1 tablespoon turbinado sugar to embellish discretionary

Directions
1. Preheat the stove to 350ºF. Line a portion dish with material paper and put away.
2. Add the dry fixings to the bowl and rush to consolidate. In a different bowl, beat together the eggs, pounded banana, oil, syrup, vinegar and vanilla and beat until smooth.
3. Pour the wet fixings into the dry and overlap together. When consolidated, overlay in the apple and walnuts.
4. Transfer hitter to the readied portion tin, sprinkle with extra slashed walnuts and turbinado sugar (if utilizing). Prepare on the middle rack for 45 - 50 minutes until the top has become brilliant earthy colored and a cake analyzer embedded into the middle confesses all.
5. Cool in the search for gold hour at that point move to a wire rack and cool totally prior to cutting.

15. Vegetarian Stuffed Sweet Potatoes with Mediterranean Quinoa

Planning Time 5 minutes | Cook Time 45 minutes | All out Time 50 minutes | Servings 2

Fixings
- 2 medium yams
- 1 tablespoon olive oil
- 2 cups spinach
- 1/2 cup canned chickpeas
- 1/4 cup sun-dried tomatoes (slashed)
- 2 tablespoons kalamata olives (slashed)
- 1 cup cooked quinoa
- 1/2 teaspoon dried thyme
- 1/2 teaspoon dried dill
- 1/2 teaspoon garlic powder
- Salt and pepper to taste
- to decorate
- 1 tablespoon tahini
- 1 teaspoon lemon juice

- Pinch of salt and pepper
- 1 - 2 tablespoons water to thin
- chives
- red pepper drops

Guidelines
1. Preheat the broiler to 400ºF. Cut the yams with a fork and spot them in a heating dish. Prepare until delicate, and blade slides into the substance effectively, around 35 – 45 minutes relying upon the size.
2. Meanwhile, set up the quinoa combination by warming the oil in a sauté skillet over medium warmth. Add the remainder of the fixings (spinach to salt and pepper) and sauté until warm. Keep warm until the yams are cooked.
3. When the yams are delicate, eliminate them from the broiler and let them cool for a couple of moments. Once cooled, move them to a plate, split them open with a sharp blade and spoon the quinoa into the middle.
4. Whisk together the tahini, lemon, salt, pepper, and water at that point pour on top of yams. Embellishment with new chives and red pepper chips. Serve quickly and appreciate.

16. Spice Crusted Tofu

Planning Time 10 minutes | Cook Time 40 minutes | All out Time 50 minutes | Servings 6

Fixings
- 2 square additional firm tofu (28 oz.)
- 2 tablespoons olive oil
- ¼ cup quinoa flour
- ½ cup wholesome yeast
- 1 tablespoon Italian flavoring
- 1 teaspoon dried garlic
- 1 teaspoon dried sage
- ¼ tsp. smoked paprika
- salt and pepper to taste

Directions
1. Preheat the stove to 400ºF.
2. Cut the tofu into steaks, around 1/2" thick. Each square ought to get you around 6 steaks. Put away.
3. In shallow bowl or dish, whisk together the dry

Fixings.
1. Now, set up your mechanical production system! Put the olive oil in another shallow dish. To start with, coat a tofu steak in oil.
2. At that point place the tofu in the bowl of the dry fixings and coat the tofu with the dry combination. Spot the steak on a heating sheet and rehash with the remainder of the tofu.
3. When prepared to heat, place the preparing sheet in the stove. Cook for 15 minutes, at that point flip and cook for another 15 - 20. You need the tofu to be brilliant earthy colored and firm.
4. Serve tofu with your 1 sauce (I love a garlic tahini sauce!) and your number one vegetable side dish. Appreciate!

17. Solid Blueberry Muffins

Planning Time 15 minutes | Cook Time 25 minutes | Absolute Time 40 minutes | Servings 9

Fixings
- for the biscuits:
- 1 flax egg (1 tbsp. flaxseed feast + 3 tbsp. water or ordinary egg)
- 1/2 cup pounded banana (around 1 medium)
- 1/2 cup fruit purée
- 1/4 cup maple syrup
- 1/4 cup non-dairy milk
- 1 1/4 cups oat flour (produced using ground oats)
- 1/2 cup quinoa drops
- 1/2 cup almond flour
- 2 teaspoons preparing powder
- 1 teaspoon cinnamon
- 1/4 teaspoon ocean salt

- 2/3 cup new blueberries
- for the coating:
- 1/4 cup coconut margarine
- 1/2 teaspoon blueberry powder

Guidelines

1. Preheat the broiler to 350ºF. Line a biscuit tin with paper liners (or oil with coconut oil) and put away.
2. Beat together wet fixings in a huge blending bowl. Add dry (less the blueberries) and mix together until joined. Overlap in the blueberries.
3. Divide player equitably between the biscuit cups (this formula makes around 9 - 10 biscuits). Heat on the middle rack for 20 - 23 minutes until a cake analyzer embedded into the middle confesses all.
4. Allow biscuits to cool in the prospect minutes at that point move to a wire rack and cool totally.
5. Once cooled, make the coating. Liquefy the coconut margarine over a twofold evaporator until it's smooth and runny. Race in blueberry powder and sprinkle over biscuits. Sprinkle each with a touch more blueberry powder whenever wanted and appreciate!

18. Cushy Flourless Peanut Butter Chickpea Muffins

Planning time 10 minutes | Cook time 25 minutes | All out time 35 minutes | Serves 10

Fixings
- 1 (15 ounce) can BUSH'S® Organic Garbanzo Beans, flushed and depleted (chickpeas)
- 3 enormous eggs
- 1/2 cup velvety normal peanut butter (just peanuts + salt)
- 1/2 cup unadulterated maple syrup (or sub nectar)
- 1 teaspoon vanilla concentrate
- 1 teaspoon heating powder
- ¼ teaspoon salt
- 1/3 cup dim chocolate chips, in addition to 2 tablespoons for sprinkling on top (without dairy, whenever wanted)

Guidelines
1. Preheat broiler to 350 degrees F. Line a 12 cup biscuit tin with 10 biscuit liners (we're just making 10 biscuits) and splash within every liner with nonstick cooking shower so the liners don't adhere to the biscuits - this is significant.
2. Place chickpeas and 1 egg in the bowl of a food processor or powerful blender and cycle until beans are very much mixed.
3. Add two different eggs, peanut butter, maple syrup, and vanilla, preparing powder and salt and interaction again until smooth. Overlay in ⅓ cup chocolate chips.
4. Divide hitter uniformly among biscuit cups. Sprinkle remaining chocolate chips equally among the highest points of every biscuit player. Prepare for 25 minutes or until toothpick embedded into the center of a biscuits confesses all. Spot on a wire rack to cool for 10 minutes, at that point eliminate biscuits from tin and move to a wire rack to cool totally.
5. Keep biscuits for a day at room temperature, at that point move to refrigerator and spot in a water/air proof compartment. Makes 10 biscuits.

19. Raspberry Chocolate Chip Protein Bars

Planning Time 10 minutes | Cook Time 25 minutes | All out Time 35 minutes | Servings 16

Fixings
- 1 flax egg 1 tbsp. flaxseed feast + 3 tbsp. water
- 1 cup cooked chickpeas
- 1 cup pounded banana around 2 enormous bananas
- ¾ cup quinoa flour
- ½ cup coconut sugar
- 1 teaspoon ground cinnamon
- ½ teaspoon heating pop
- Pinch of salt
- ¼ cup hemp hearts
- ¼ cup frozen raspberries
- 1/4 cup chocolate chips

Guidelines
1. Preheat the broiler to 350°F. Oil and line a 8x8 preparing container with material and put away.
2. Whisk together the flaxseed feast and water in a little bowl. Put away for 5 minutes.
3. Once gelled, mix the flax egg, chickpeas and banana in a food processor until totally smooth.
4. Add the dry fixings (less the hemp hearts, chocolate chips and raspberries) and mix again until smooth. Heartbeat in the leftover fixings.
5. Dump the hitter into the readied container. Sprinkle with extra chocolate chips and raspberries whenever wanted and heat on the middle rack for 25 - 30 minutes until a toothpick embedded into the middle confesses all.
6. Let cool in the search for gold - 15 minutes, at that point move to a wire rack and cool totally prior to cutting.
7. Slice into 12 - 16 bars. Store in a hermetically sealed holder for 2 - 3 days.

20. One Pot Vegetable Chickpea Curry

Planning Time 10 minutes | Cook Time 40 minutes | All out Time 50 minutes | Servings 6

Fixings
- 1 tablespoon olive oil
- 1/2 cup slashed white onion around 1/2 a medium
- 4 - 5 minced garlic cloves
- 2 1/2 cups cubed butternut squash 1 little
- 2 cups broccoli florets
- 1 cup hacked ringer pepper around 1 entirety
- 1 (15 oz.) can diced tomatoes
- 1 (14.5 oz.) can light coconut milk
- 3 cups low sodium vegetable stock
- 1 (15 oz.) can chickpeas
- 1 teaspoon cumin
- 3/4 teaspoon coriander
- 2 teaspoons curry
- 1/4 teaspoon cinnamon
- 1/2 teaspoon turmeric

- Salt + pepper to taste
- 1 cup cleaved kale (discretionary)
- Cilantro to decorate
- serve with coconut lime quinoa

Guidelines

1. Heat the oil in an enormous pan or Dutch broiler. Add the onion and garlic and sauté until fragrant, around 3 minutes. Add the squash, broccoli, pepper, and chickpeas, and sauté for an additional 2 minutes.
2. Pour in the tomatoes, coconut milk, stock, and flavors and season with salt and pepper. Heat the combination to the point of boiling. When bubbling, go down to a stew and cover, cooking until squash is delicate around 30 minutes.
3. When prepared to serve, mix in kale (if utilizing) and move into bowls. Present with coconut lime quinoa and decorate with cilantro.

21. Curried Chickpea and Carrot Burgers

Planning Time 30 minutes | Cook Time 30 minutes | All out Time 60 minutes |Servings 8

Fixings
- 2 cups slashed carrots
- 1 little shallot
- 2 garlic cloves
- 1 (15oz) can chickpeas, depleted and flushed
- 2/3 cup moved oats
- 2 flax egg
- 1 tablespoon curry powder
- 1 teaspoon cumin
- 1 teaspoon smoked paprika
- Salt and pepper to taste
- 1/3 cup flaxseed dinner

Guidelines
1. Blitz the carrots, shallots and garlic in a food processor. Add the excess fixings and heartbeat to frame a mixture.
2. Divide the mixture into 8 equivalent parts and shape them into patties. Spot the burgers on a plate and refrigerate for 30 minutes.
3. When prepared to cook, preheat the stove to 375ºF.
4. Add the burgers to a material lined preparing sheet and heat for 40 minutes, flipping partially through.
5. Serve quickly (or hold up for some other time) with your number one garnishes!

22. Moroccan Chickpea Stew

Planning Time 10 minutes | Cook Time 4 hours | Complete Time 4 hours 10 minutes | Servings 6

Fixings
- 1 medium white onion hacked
- 3 garlic cloves minced
- 1 little butternut squash stripped and hacked into scaled down pieces
- 1 red chime pepper slashed
- 3/4 cup red lentils
- 1 15 oz. can chickpeas, depleted and washed
- 1 15 oz. can unadulterated pureed tomatoes
- 1 teaspoon newly ground ginger
- 1 teaspoon turmeric
- 1 teaspoon cumin
- 1 teaspoon smoked paprika
- 1/2 teaspoon cinnamon

- 1/2 teaspoon salt and pepper + more depending on the situation
- 3 cups vegetable stock
- to serve:
- cooked quinoa
- arugula
- coconut yogurt

Guidelines

1. Add all fixings to a lethargic cooker. Mix together to join, at that point cover and cook on high for 3 - 4 hours (or 6 - 7 hours on low).
2. For a thicker stew, eliminate the cover with 1 hour left in cooking.
3. Serve with quinoa, a small bunch of arugula and a touch of yogurt.

23. Curry Chickpea Lettuce Wraps

Planning Time 5 minutes | Complete Time 5 minutes | Servings 2

Fixings
- 1/4 cup coconut yogurt
- 1 tablespoon tahini
- 1 tablespoon lemon juice
- 1 - 2 teaspoons curry powder
- 1/2 teaspoon garlic powder
- 1/2 teaspoon ocean salt
- 1/4 teaspoon new pepper
- Water as need to thin
- 1 can chickpeas depleted and washed
- 2 tablespoons cleaved parsley
- 2 tablespoons cleaved scallions
- 1 head spread lettuce or Boston face cloth, romaine, collards, and so forth
- Tahini to shower

Directions
1. In a little bowl, combine as one yogurt, tahini, lemon squeeze and flavors until smooth. Add water 1 tablespoon at a time until the blend is pourable.
2. Add chickpeas to a blending bowl, alongside 1 tablespoon of the dressing, and squash them with a fork until the vast majority of the chickpeas are squashed. Mix in the leftover dressing, parsley and scallions until joined.
3. Divide chickpea salad equitably between lettuce leaves and shower with a touch of tahini (if desired).

24. Quinoa Greek Salad with Chickpeas

Planning Time 10 minutes | Refrigerate 30 minutes | All out Time 40 minutes | Servings 6

Fixings
- 3 cups cooked quinoa cooled totally
- 1 15 oz. can natural chickpeas, depleted and flushed
- 1 medium cucumber quartered and slashed
- 1 red onion diced
- 1 cup cherry tomatoes quartered
- 1/2 cup kalamata olives pitted and diced
- 1/2 cup level leaf parsley slashed
- Juice of 2 lemons
- 2 tablespoons olive oil
- 2 tablespoons Dijon mustard
- Salt and pepper to taste

Guidelines
1. Toss the quinoa, chickpeas and veggies together in an enormous bowl. Add the parsley throw to join.

2. Whisk together the lemon, olive oil, Dijon mustard, salt and pepper until smooth. Pour over the serving of mixed greens and throw together. Taste and change salt and pepper if necessary.
3. Chill in the ice chest for at any rate 30 minutes, ideally for 60 minutes, at that point serve.

25. Simmered Vegetable Quinoa Salad

Planning Time 15 minutes | Cook Time 30 minutes | All out Time 45 minutes | Servings 8

Fixings

- for the plate of mixed greens:
- 1 cups uncooked quinoa
- 2 cups water
- 2 cups cauliflower florets
- 1 cup Brussels sprouts split
- 1 cup green beans stemmed and split
- 1 tablespoon olive oil
- 1 15 oz. jars natural chickpeas, washed
- 1/4 cup sunflower seeds
- 1/4 cup pumpkin seeds
- Salt and pepper to taste
- for the dressing:
- 1 teaspoon coriander seeds
- 1 teaspoon cumin seeds
- 1 teaspoon fennel seeds
- 1/4 cup olive oil
- 1/4 cup white wine vinegar

- Juice of one lemons
- Large touch of salt and pepper

Directions
1. Preheat stove to 425ºF.
2. Toss vegetables with the olive oil and sprinkle with salt and pepper. Spot on a preparing sheet and meal until delicate, 25 - 30 mins.
3. While veggies are broiling, cook quinoa. Add quinoa and water into a sauce dish. Heat to the point of boiling, cover and lessen to stew for 15 minutes. When cooked, eliminate from warmth and let sit, covered for 5 minutes.
4. After cooling, move quinoa to a preparing sheet and refrigerate until cool, around 20 mins.
5. While quinoa is cooling and veggies are broiling, set up the vinaigrette. Toast coriander, cumin and fennel seeds in a dry skillet over medium warmth until fragrant, around 2 - 3 minutes. Give cool at that point hack or crush access a flavor processor.
6. Whisk flavors with residual fixings and put vinaigrette away.
7. When veggies are finished cooking and quinoa has cooled, move them all to a huge serving bowl. Add chickpeas, sunflower seeds, and pumpkin seeds and throw to join. Sprinkle with vinaigrette and throw until covered. Taste and change flavors as wanted.

8. Serve chilled or somewhat warmed. What's more, obviously, kindly appreciate!

26. Simmered Vegetable Quinoa Salad

Planning Time 5 minutes| Absolute Time 5 minutes | Servings 2

Fixings
- for the plate of mixed greens
- 1 cup canned chickpeas
- 1 cup slashed cucumbers
- 1 cup slashed cherry tomatoes
- 1 cup cooked quinoa
- 1/2 cup slashed level leaf parsley
- 3 - 4 cups arugula
- for the dressing
- 2 tablespoon olive oil
- Juice of 1 lemon
- 1 teaspoon Dijon mustard
- 1 teaspoon maple syrup
- 1/2 teaspoon garlic powder
- Salt and pepper to taste

Directions
1. Begin with the dressing. Whisk all fixings together in a little bowl. Taste and change preparing whenever wanted.
2. When prepared to gather the plates of mixed greens, uniformly split the dressing between 2 wide-mouth bricklayer containers (quart size). At that point equitably partition the leftover fixings and add to the artisan containers in the request recorded. Seal with cover and store in the fridge until prepared to eat.
3. When serving, pour substance of the artisan container into a bowl. Mix around to help get dressing disseminated and appreciate!

27. Tofu Roll in a Bowl

Planning Time 5 minutes | Cook Time 15 minutes | Absolute Time 20 minutes | Servings 2

Fixings
- 1 square (14oz) very firm tofu
- 2 tablespoons avocado oil/olive oil
- 1/2 white onion , diced (around 1 cup)
- 3 garlic cloves , minced
- 1/4 cup tamari/soy sauce , separated
- 1 bundle coleslaw blend (12-14oz)
- 1 head wavy kale (around 3 cups hacked)
- 2 tablespoons rice wine vinegar
- 1-2 teaspoons sriracha hot sauce
- 2 teaspoon toasted sesame oil
- 1/2 pack scallions , meagerly cut (around 3 - 4 scallions)
- Water on a case by case basis

Directions
1. Heat 1 tablespoon of oil in a huge skillet. Cut the tofu into 1" solid shapes and add it to the dish. Cook for 3 - 4 minutes for every side until it's fresh.
2. While the tofu is cooking, heat the second tablespoon of oil in a different container. When hot, add the garlic and onion, and sauté for 2 - 3 minutes until delicate. Gather the ginger and two tablespoons of tamari and mix into a single unit.
3. Add the coleslaw blend and kale and sauté until everything has shriveled. Add a tablespoon or two of water during the cooking interaction to help it steam.
4. Once mellowed, add the tofu, the excess tamari, rice vinegar, hot sauce, toasted sesame oil, and scallions. Cook for one more moment or so until everything is consolidated and delightful.
5. Serve promptly with a couple of additional scallions and some sesame seeds.

28. Coconut Matcha Oatmeal

Cook Time 5 minutes | All out Time 5 minutes | Servings 2

Fixings
- 1 1/2 cups water
- 1 1/2 cups coconut water
- 1 cup moved oats
- 2 tablespoons coconut flour
- 2 tablespoons maple syrup
- 2 teaspoons matcha powder
- 1/4 cup destroyed coconut

Guidelines
1. Add water, coconut water and oats into a little pan. Carry the waters to bubble, lessen to stew and keep on mixing until the blend starts to thicken, around 1 moment.
2. Stir in coconut flour, syrup and matcha. Proceed to cook and mix until the blend has

arrived at your ideal consistency. Overlay in the destroyed coconut.
3. Divide similarly between two dishes. Top with your garnishes of decision!

29. No Bake High Protein Funfetti Bars

Time 30 minutes | Serves 10

Fixings
- 1 1/4 cup oat flour gluten free, if needed*
- 1/4 cup cake flour can utilize all oat flour*
- 1/4 cup coconut flour
- 2 scoops vanilla protein powder See 'search' for my suggestions Optional
- pinch ocean salt
- Granulated sugar of choice
- 1/2 tsp. vanilla concentrate
- 1/2 cup nut spread of decision I utilized both drippy almond margarine and drippy cashew spread
- 1/2 cup earthy colored rice syrup sub for nectar or maple syrup for paleo alternative
- 1 T + milk of choice
- Sprinkles discretionary

Directions
1. Line a 9 x 9 preparing dish with material paper and put away.
2. In a huge blending bowl, consolidate your flours, protein powder, ocean salt and granulated sugar and put away.
3. In a microwave safe bowl or burner, dissolve your nut margarine with the earthy colored rice syrup (or maple/nectar). Rush in the vanilla concentrate and fill the dry blend. Blend very well until completely fused.
4. If hitter is excessively thick (it by and large is), add a tablespoon of milk or more, until a thick player is framed. In the event that hitter is excessively meager, add a scramble more flour until a thick player is shaped. Mix in discretionary sprinkles and move hitter to lined heating dish and press immovably into it.
5. Refrigerate for in any event 10 minutes, or until firm.

30. Veggie lover Strawberry Cheese Cake

Planning time 10 minutes | Cook time 25 minutes | Absolute time 35 minutes | Serves 5

Fixings:
- Cake base fixings:
- 1 1/2 cups of moved oats
- 1 1/2 cups of ground almonds
- 1/3 cup of coconut oil
- 1 tsp. vanilla concentrate
- 4 tbsp. agave nectar (or maple syrup)
- Cheddar cake fixings:
- 400ml of canned full fat coconut milk
- 350g smooth tofu
- 300 - 350g strawberries (more for adorning)
- 5 tbsp. agave nectar (or maple syrup)
- 1 tsp. vanilla concentrate
- 5g agar powder

Strategy:
1. Preheat your stove to 180C (360F).
2. Add all cake base fixings to a food processor and mix for about 45 seconds. You ought to get a brittle batter that remains together without any problem.
3. Line a preparing tin with heating paper.
4. Add the cake base batter to the tin and even it out so you get a pleasant level and surprisingly base.
5. Bake in the stove for 15 minutes.
6. In the interim add all cheddar cake fixings to a blender and mix until you get a smooth combination.
7. Pour the cheddar cake blend into a skillet, heat up and cook for 3-4 minutes. This is significant as the agar powder should be warmed up first before it can make the cheddar cake set. Ensure you mix constantly so it doesn't consume.
8. Take the cheddar cake combination off the warmth and pour it on top the cake base in the heating tin you just prepared. The cake base and preparing paper should keep the fluid fixed.
9. Now it's tied in with allowing it to set, so you need to allow it to chill off totally for a couple of hours. Or then again far superior, put it into the cooler and let cool down for at any rate 2 hours. It needs some time to totally set and it likewise tastes much better when it's chilled.
10. When it has set remove the preparing ring and beautify with strawberries. Enjoy!

31. Chickpea Oat Patties

Planning time 10 minutes | Cook time 25 minutes | Complete time 35 minutes | Serves 7

Fixings (2 segments):
- Chickpea oat patties fixings:
- 1/2 cup gram flour (chickpea flour)
- 1/2 cup water
- 1/2 tsp. turmeric powder
- 1/2 tsp. garlic powder/granules
- 1/2 tsp. salt
- 1/2 tsp. bar-b-que preparing
- 1/2 cup oats
- Pistachio chreme fixings:
- 100g pistachios
- 1/2 stock solid shape
- 1/2 tsp. garlic powder/granules
- 1 tsp. additional virgin olive oil
- 1 tsp. lemon juice

- Different fixings:
- 2 Portobello mushrooms
- 1 fennel

Strategy:
1. Start with blending the gram flour and water with a whisk (or a fork may do too in the event that you don't care about it taking somewhat more) until you get a smooth combination. At that point add any remaining chickpea oat patty fixings and continue to blend well until it turns into an uncooked blend.
2. Heat up some oil in a container and spot an enormous spoonful of mixture into the skillet and smooth it with the spoon to make patty shapes. Fry well on the two sides.
3. If you have an enormous enough dish likewise add the mushroom (season first with a touch of salt and garlic powder) and slash up the fennel and fry (the mushroom will presumably take the longest to mellow). In any case fry them independently.
4. In the interim put all fixings into a blender with a touch of water (ensure you save a couple of pistachio bits for improvement) and mix well until you get a smooth creme.
5. Only add the water gradually so the creme doesn't get excessively fluid. Relies upon how pungent you like it you should add a touch of salt to taste.
6. 8.   When everything is done plate the chickpea oat patties first, at that point the mushroom, fennel and ultimately the pistachio creme on top. Cleave up a portion of the

pistachio pieces and sprinkle them over your creation. Appreciate!

32. Veggie lover Pancakes Special

Planning time 10 minutes | Cook time 20 minutes | Complete time 30 minutes | Serves 10

Fixings (2 flapjacks):

Fixings flapjack:
- 1/4 cup of self-raising whole meal flour
- 1/4 cup of gram flour (chickpea flour)
- 3/4 Cup of soy milk or any plant-based milk
- 1/4 tsp. salt
- 1/4 tsp. garlic powder/granules
- **Fixings filling:**
- 1 little avocado
- 1 little courgette (zucchini)
- Some dill
- 1 tbsp. lemon juice

- Some garlic (or garlic powder/granules)
- Soy sauce
- Hummus any

METHOD:
1. Start with cutting deseeding an avocado and cut into little blocks and put away. Do likewise with the courgette and fry in a touch of oil, lemon juice, soy sauce and garlic.
2. Once they mollify turn down the warmth and add some new sliced dill to it. Put away too.
3. Now either whisk all hotcake fixings in a bowl or in the event that you feel lethargic like me simply join, in a little blender.
4. Add some oil to a non-stick container (ensure the entire surface is covered, you can spread the oil in the dish with a kitchen towel), change the hob to medium warmth and empty portion of the combination into the skillet. Ensure it's just a slight layer.
5. Fry on the two sides (flip them like you would with flapjacks).
1. 8. When they are done put them on a level surface.
2. 9. In the hotcakes add hummus, the dill courgettes and avocado in succession. Overlay over the highest point of the hotcake and move it in.
3. 10. Serve in its own or with a plate of mixed greens as an afterthought. Appreciate!

33. Broiled Red Pepper Pizza

Planning time 30 minutes | Cook time 30 minutes | Complete time an hour | Serves 10

Fixings
For the Roasted Red Pepper Pizza:
- Pizza Dough, hand crafted or locally acquired
- 1/2 cup Tomato Sauce
- 2 teaspoon Italian Seasoning
- Pinch of Salt and Pepper
- Vegan Mozzarella Cheese
- 1 Roasted Red Pepper, from container
- 6-7 Cherry or Grape Tomatoes
- 2-3 Garlic Cloves, daintily cut
- Fresh Basil
- Olive Oil, for brushing on outside
- For the Tofu Ricotta:
- Half a Block of Extra Firm Tofu
- 1 tablespoon Lemon Juice
- 1/2 teaspoon Apple Cider Vinegar
- 2 tablespoon Nutritional Yeast

- 1/4-1/2 teaspoon Salt
- Pinch of Black Pepper
- For the Balsamic Glaze:
- 1/2 cup Balsamic Vinegar
- 1 tablespoon Brown Sugar

Arrangement
1. For the Pizza:
   1. If you have a most loved pizza batter formula, utilize that! If not, locally acquired functions admirably!
   2. Preheat stove to 425F.
   3. Add the pureed tomatoes to a little bowl and blend in the Italian flavors, salt, and pepper. Spread the pureed tomatoes on the pizza batter.
   4. Sprinkle so much or as little veggie lover mozzarella cheddar on top of the pureed tomatoes as you'd like.
   5. Thinly cut the cooked red pepper, cherry tomatoes, and garlic. Make certain to leave the garlic in greater pieces or cuts so it doesn't consume. Uniformly spread garnishes on the pizza.
   6. Add the tofu, lemon juice, apple juice vinegar, wholesome yeast, salt, and pepper to a food processor.
   7. Pulse until smooth yet has some surface. Dab spoonfuls equitably on the pizza.
2. For the Assemble and Bake:
   1. Brush the pizza hull with olive oil and sprinkle with garlic powder and salt whenever wanted.

2. Bake the pizza for 20-25 minutes or until the hull is brilliant earthy colored. Each stove is unique so watch out for it.
3. While the pizza is cooking, make the balsamic coating. Add the balsamic vinegar and earthy colored sugar in to a little pot.
4. Bring to a bubble and afterward decrease to a stew. Cook until the balsamic coating has decreased and thickened. It should cover the rear of a spoon. Around 10-15 minutes.

34. High Protein Spinach and Rice Balls

Planning time 10 minutes | Cook time 25 minutes | Complete time 35 minutes | Serves 10

Fixings
To Make Part One:
- 4 1/2 cups spinach leaves
- 1/3 cup pitted Greek olives
- 1 tablespoon dietary yeast
- 1 tablespoon lemon juice
- 1 teaspoon garlic powder
- 3/4 teaspoon salt
- To Make Part Two:
- 1 1/4 cup cooked rice
- 1/2 cup ground almonds
- 1/2 cup chickpea flour
- To Serve Over:
- Cashew harsh cream or coconut yogurt

Planning

1. Preheat your broiler to 360°F.
2. Add all elements of section 1 into a food processor and mix.
3. Then exchange the combination into a huge bowl and blend in the elements of section 2. Combine as one well until you get a decent batter like surface. In the event that it's too wet add somewhat more chickpea flour. Try not to taste it now as uncooked chickpea flour is exceptionally unpleasant. Add pepper to taste also on the off chance that you like.
4. Create approximately 12 balls with your gives (it's somewhat muddled however fun) and spot on a preparing plate fixed with heating paper. Put into the preheated broiler and heat for 20 - 25 min (likely 20 min will do, you can check by tasting one of them, assuming there could be no unpleasant taste to it, it's ideal).
5. Serve over cashew acrid cream or coconut yogurt.

35. Lentil Quinoa Seed balls

Planning time 15 minutes | Cook time 25 minutes | All out time 40 minutes | Serves 10

Fixings
- 1 cup cooked red lentils, depleted well
- 1/2 cup cooked quinoa
- 3 tablespoons sun-dried tomatoes, slashed
- 1 tablespoon ground flax seed
- 2-3 tablespoons hemp seeds
- 1 tablespoon sans gluten oat flour
- 1 tablespoon wholesome yeast
- 1 teaspoon oregano, or to taste
- 1/2 teaspoon garlic powder
- 1/2 teaspoon onion powder
- 1/4 teaspoon ocean salt, or to taste
- 1/8 teaspoon dark pepper, or to taste
- 1/2-3/4 cup sans gluten bread morsels

Planning
1. Combine all fixings aside from bread scraps in a food processor and heartbeat them around 6-8 times, until they're joined.
2. Add the breadcrumbs to a shallow bowl.
3. Use a tablespoon to scoop out the bean combination and utilize your hand to form some into a ball. You can't actually move them in your grasp; tenderly shape them.
4. Then, coat the bean balls in the scraps by delicately squeezing and folding them into the morsels.
5. If you need to sear them, add around 1/2 tablespoon of coconut oil to a skillet and warmth it over medium warmth until a morsel threw in the oil sizzles quickly on contact. Add the bean balls and cook, turning over at regular intervals until they're brilliant and warmed through.
6. If you need to prepare them, Pre-heat broiler to 400°F. Spot meatballs on a material lined preparing sheet and heat them for around 15 minutes, or until daintily seared.

36. The Green Warrior Burger

Planning Time: 20 minutes | Cook Time: 10 minutes | All out Time: 30 minutes | Yield: 4 burgers

Fixings
- For the green burger patties:
- 1 onion
- 1/2 cup moved oats (check if GF)
- 1/2 cup spinach
- 1/2 cup new parsley
- 1/2 cup new basil
- 2 cups garden peas (cooked)
- 1 can margarine beans (400 g/240 g depleted)
- salt and pepper to taste
- olive oil for cooking
- For the burger:
- 1 mozzarella or vegetarian cheddar (discretionary)
- 4 bread rolls

- a few tbsp. of sun-dried tomato pesto (check if vegetarian)
- 1 avocado
- spinach/lettuce or potentially salad cress

Directions
1. Cook the nursery peas in bubbled water for only 2-5 minutes or as long as the directions on the bundle say. Leave them to cool or essentially wash with cold water; don't put them in the food processor while they are as yet hot.
2. In a food processor mix the onion with the oats.
3. Add the remainder of the elements for the patties: the new mixed greens, the margarine beans, the peas and preparing. Mix until you get a tacky, smooth green blend like the one in the video.
4. Shape the blend into burger patties and brush each side with olive oil.
5. Heat a non-stick dish to medium warmth, sprinkle a tiny bit of piece of olive oil and spot the patties in the skillet, cooking each side for 4-5 minutes.
6. When one side is cooked and you flip the patties, place a cut of mozzarella or veggie lover cheddar on top and cover with a top while the opposite side is cooking, to permit it dissolve.
7. Serve the patties in a burger with new spinach or other serving of mixed greens (like cress), sun-dried tomato pesto and avocado.

37. Messy Vegan Protein Pasta

Planning time 6 minutes | Cook time 7 minutes | All out time 13 minutes | Serving 2/3

Fixings
- 1 can White beans, 15oz/400g
- 2½ cups/160g Bean/Lentil Pasta
- 4 tbsp. Nutritional yeast
- ½ cup/120ml Water
- 1 Garlic clove
- 2 tbsp. Sesame seeds
- ¼ tsp. Turmeric
- 1 tbsp. Apple juice vinegar
- ½ tsp. Smoked Paprika
- ½ tsp. Chopped Basil
- pinch of Salt and Pepper

Guidelines
1. Drain the beans and spot everything separated from the pasta into a blender and whizz until consolidated.
2. Cook the pasta according to guidelines and channel.
3. Stir in the messy bean pasta sauce.

4. Serve with smoked paprika and basil sprinkled on top.
5. Store extras in the cooler and appreciate inside three days.

38. Tofu Scramble

Planning time 10 minutes | Cook time 25 minutes | Complete time 35 minutes | Makes 4 servings

Fixings
- tofu, additional firm (light or low-fat whenever the situation allows) (14-16 ounces)
- garlic, minced (1 clove)
- onion, diced (1/2 cup)
- green pepper, diced (1/2 cup)
- red pepper, diced (1/2 cup)
- mushrooms, hacked (3/4 cup)
- turmeric powder (1/4 teaspoon)
- cumin powder (1 teaspoon)
- black pepper (3/4 teaspoon)
- salt (1 teaspoon)

Bearings
1. Add 1/4 cup water to huge sauté container. When warmed, add onion.
2. When the fragrance discharges from the onion and it begins to get clear, add garlic.

Cook for 2 minutes, add peppers and mushrooms and add 1/4 cup water if vegetables are adhering to the container. Cook for around 4 minutes or until vegetables are delicate.
3. Crumble tofu with hands and add to dish alongside turmeric, blending admirably. Add cumin powder, pepper, and salt, and cook for another 4-6 minutes until everything is cooked through.
4. Serve with entire grain toast or on a warm corn tortilla.

39. Sesame-Ginger Chickpea Cakes

Planning time 15 minutes | Cook time 20 minutes | Complete time 35 minutes | Serves: 6-8 patties

Fixings
- For the chickpea cakes:
- 3 tablespoons extra-virgin olive oil, separated
- 1 shallot, hacked
- 1 tablespoon soy sauce
- 1 garlic clove, minced
- 1 cup cooked chickpeas, somewhat pounded with a fork
- 2 scallions, white and green parts, hacked
- ½ tablespoon ground new ginger
- 1 teaspoon sesame oil
- 2 eggs, tenderly whisked
- ½ teaspoon dried coriander
- ¼ cup hacked cilantro
- 1 cup panko breadcrumbs
- A few squeezes sesame seeds

- Sea salt and new dark pepper
- For the yogurt sauce:
- Heaping ½ cup plain yogurt
- 1 tablespoon extra-virgin olive oil
- 1 teaspoon agave or nectar
- 1 teaspoon minced onion or a couple of squeezes onion powder
- ½ garlic clove, minced
- 1 tablespoon new lime juice, in addition to some zing
- ½ teaspoon earthy colored mustard seeds
- ¼ cup cleaved cilantro
- Sea salt

Directions

1. Heat 1 tablespoon of the olive oil in a little skillet. Add the shallots and cook for a couple of moments on medium warmth until clear. Mood killer the warmth and add the soy sauce and garlic.
2. Stir together in the hot search for gold moment. Put away.
3. In a medium bowl, join the chickpeas, scallions, ginger, sesame oil, eggs, coriander, cilantro, and cooked shallots. Structure into little or medium measured patties (6 medium, or 8 little).
4. I think that its simplest to attempt to pack them into a ball and afterward tenderly press down to smooth.
5. They will self-destruct effectively, so attempt to pat them together admirably well. Spot them in the ice chest while you combine the sauce as one, at any rate 15-30 minutes.

6. Make the yogurt sauce: In a little bowl, mix together the yogurt, olive oil, agave, onion, garlic, lime juice, mustard seeds, cilantro, and a touch of salt.
7. Taste and change flavors. Chill until prepared to serve.
8. Spread the panko on a plate or level surface and blend in a couple of portions of salt, pepper, and sesame seeds.
9. Roll every patty in the panko blend, covering generously, and put each away.
10. Heat the excess 2 tablespoons of olive oil in an enormous skillet (be certain the lower part of your skillet is totally covered with the oil so your cakes don't come out dry).
11. When the oil is extremely hot, add the patties. Cook for 1-2 minutes on each side, or until brilliant earthy colored. Present with the yogurt sauce.

40. Dalgona Whipped Matcha

Planning Time 5 minute's |Absolute Time 5 minutes |Servings 4

Fixings
- Liquid from 1 (15oz) jar of chickpeas
- 1 tablespoon matcha powder
- 2 tablespoons coconut sugar
- 2 tablespoons bubbling water
- 4 cups almond milk

Guidelines
1. Add the chickpea fluid into a stand blender (or bowl).
2. Using the whisk connection beat the fluid until it shapes firm pinnacles. It should require about a little while.
3. In a different bowl, whisk together the matcha, coconut sugar
4. And bubbling water to attempt to disintegrate the sugar precious stones

however much as could reasonably be expected.
5. Once disintegrated, walk out on medium speed and gradually empty the matcha-sugar combination into the bowl.
6. Beat together until everything is consolidated.
7. Fill your glasses with ice and top each with 1 cup of almond milk. Top with the whipped matcha, give it a fast mix and appreciate!
8. Transfer hitter to the lined 8×8 heating skillet and spread the player out equitably.
9. Sprinkle with ocean salt and additional cinnamon on top.
10. Bake for 25-30 minutes, until blade embedded confesses all and edges are brilliant earthy colored.
11. Baking occasions shift, contingent upon what sugar/flour you use.
12. If edges are beginning to brown and the center isn't done, at that point cover the container with foil and keep heating until focus is completely prepared.

Conclusion

Finally, I might want to thank you for picking this book. This incorporates recipes for athletes who need healthy food and these are not difficult to plan at home and are wealthy in supplements. These recipes can be effortlessly set up inside less time. These recipes are palatable and mind blowing. Attempt at home and appreciate.

I wish you all good luck!

CPSIA information can be obtained
at www.ICGtesting.com
Printed in the USA
BVHW091723310521
608479BV00009B/1661